Jellybeans
FROM HEAVEN

Jellybeans
FROM HEAVEN

DR. SYLVIA TRAYMORE MORRISON

purposely
created
PUBLISHING

JELLYBEANS FROM HEAVEN

Published by Purposely Created Publishing Group™
Copyright © 2018 Sylvia Traymore Morrison
All rights reserved.

Unless otherwise indicated, scripture quotations are from the Holy Bible, King James Version. All rights reserved.

Printed in the United States of America

ISBN: 978-1-947054-82-0

Special discounts are available on bulk quantity purchases by book clubs, associations and special interest groups. For details email: sales@publishyourgift.com or call (888) 949-6228.
For information logon to: www.PublishYourGift.com

Dedication

For John and Betty Mae Dabney Morrison – Thanks for all your jellybeans.

Daddy, I know you dropped a few. And Ma, thanks for that green one. It was awesome! I miss you both and not one day goes by without you in my thoughts.

For Wansley Pitt, Robert Walters, and Shebah Aqeel – Thanks for all the memories and jellybeans. I miss you guys unlike anything you would know. I am sure Heaven is rejoicing with you. Your work with the jellybeans has been incredible.

Michael Raibman, thank you. Your hard work (jellybean) saved my life. Literally.

Table of Contents

To God

Thank you for this project in its entirety. It has been nothing but a blessing since the day you put it in my heart to perform on stage. It is simply, in my opinion, one of the greatest gifts/works with which you have blessed me. Thank you again and again. And then, again and again.

Acknowledgments

————✦————

As a young child, I used to wonder why God did not make me special.

I grew up such an insecure little soul. I admired what everybody else had or could do, and I had no confidence in myself whatsoever.

I used to wish I was beautiful, wish I could draw or paint. I wanted to play music on instruments and be just as good as a couple of my friends. I wanted to sing. I wanted to play basketball, ping-pong, or tennis. I wanted to be a spelling bee winner. I dreamed of becoming the best lawyer in the world. How about if I was a school-teacher? I wanted to be smart and not have to study like some of my naturally smart friends. I wanted to be a high fashion model, be able to play baseball, football, or become a fighter (I got beat up a few times, so I let that one go). I thought of dancing – being a ballerina, or a tap dancer, or maybe I could be a judge in a courtroom, or how about a preacher? I wanted to be special, simply because everyone I knew was special.

Everybody but me.

I always came in second or third place, never the leader. I could not understand why I was the only one I knew who had to always take a back seat.

Whenever I saw one of my friends excel at something, I wanted to do it too. I wanted to be special like almost everybody I knew, but I felt like a little black sheep.

Then, one day, the revelation showed up. My life changed. While I loved it, I did not know what a big gift it was.

The little insecure person who grew up thinking everyone had something special except for her, found her niche! It made me shine and want to share the gift with the world! I was the only person I knew who could do what I did. Others tried to do what I did just like I tried to do what they did. It hit me. God made me special too. As a matter of fact, it occurred to me that he made everybody special.

I was not supposed to be a sports figure or a musician who played an instrument. I was not supposed to be the greatest double Dutch jumper, nor was I supposed to be a famous dancer.

For this, I would like to thank God again. He put me here at a time when I was the only black female sharing my specialty with the world. I could have cared less about the discrimination and gender barriers. All I wanted to do was share what I did.

Being turned down over and over while pursuing a dream can be quite a challenge. Being told you are horrible, bad, not talented, not wanted, you need to find something else to do, and you name it, can be damaging. It was damaging. I didn't care. I just wanted to do what I absolutely loved. Point blank.

I remember overlooking everything—the words, actions, and despicable atmosphere I was exposed to yet never, not once, wanting to give up. The passion was deep in my soul and no matter what, I was down for whatever was coming my way.

Thank you, Lord, for giving me that heart. I sincerely appreciate it.

I would also like to thank my daughters, Jasmin and Michelle. They have been on this journey with me all their lives. Not once did they complain that I was "doing too much" or worked too hard at home and away. They basically did not care. If I was happy they were good. I honestly don't know what I did to deserve these two, but I think God said, "The journey is going to be tough, so I'm going to give you two little people who will make you smile at just the sight of them." And that's what happened.

Jasmin and Michelle, when you read this, I want you to know just how much I absolutely love you. You not only made life worth living, you gave me life. I'm so thankful for the two of you.

I don't want to forget my grandchildren, Kamryn, K.J., Kiley, and Duke (they were born in that order). The last three are the same age, two are twins and I love them madly. Duke was born just two months after the twins. He warms my heart. His smile is unmistakable in his love for me and I love him. Kamryn is the oldest and my jewel. She simply shines in my heart and I love her. The twins are like prizes. K.J. and Kiley are like two little suns. They light up my world.

When I tell you grandchildren are special, I already know that many of you know exactly what I mean. After my own girls were born, I couldn't imagine loving like that again until I met the grands. I love you guys. Oh, how I love you.

I'd like to thank my siblings. As the youngest, I was always entertained by their silliness. We've had our times, but they've made me realize that even amid the dark, light is on its way. Thank you Jerry, Chubby, Peter, Jacky, and Poochie. You are so crazy, and I love you!

I would like to shout out two of my personal jellybeans, Sandy Halmon and Betty Entzminger. God bless you both. I honestly don't know what I would have done without you two at times. Thank you for always being a blessing.

Iwari DeWees and Najah Haquiqah, I believe you guys started the social network kicking for me. That whole Muhammad Ali experience was made real once God brought you into my life. Thank you so much. You guys are awesome jellybeans!

Finally, for all the friends I have who for years had no clue what I do and still embraced me, thank you. It has blessed my heart.

I pray somewhere down the line, someone drops a jellybean on you!

Introduction

————•◦❋◦•————

When this storyline first came to mind, it came all at once. There was no sitting down, thinking about it, writing it out, etc. I knew exactly what it was supposed to be. I was thinking of a tribute to Whitney Houston since she had been instrumental in my career growth. Her memory played a huge role in my performances. She inspired the stage performance, which eventually led to the writing of this book.

To all who read this book, I pray you enjoy my interpretation of what happens when you arrive in Heaven. Of course, I don't know what really happens, but I certainly enjoy creating the stories and performing what you are about to read!

I pray that all of us, at one time or another, receive a plethora of jellybeans! Thank you so much for your support.

"In the beginning God created the heaven and the earth.

And the earth was without form, and void; and darkness was upon the face of the deep. And the Spirit of God moved upon the face of the waters.

And God said, Let there be light: and there was light.

And God saw the light, that it was good: and God divided the light from the darkness.

And God called the light Day, and the darkness he called Night. And the evening and the morning were the first day."—Genesis 1:1-5 (KJV)

Every day, Bisalten focused on what souls he could snatch. He was a soldier for the dark side. His business was serious.

Bisalten was evil. Pure evil.

The Trip

Carlie was in a deep sleep. She remembered being in a fight. A mental fight. She was pulling away from something. She did not want to go with whoever or whatever, wherever it was pulling her. She thought she was screaming, but she wasn't sure.

The fight was horrific, especially with the loud roars. There must have been three of them. They were dull brown and green in color like grass that had not been cared for. Their skin was burnt. One of them, Bisalten was his name, had a long tail that stretched for maybe 20 feet. It had sharp points. Bisalten must have been their boss because it was basically just watching. The whole time it watched, it twisted all 27 fingers on each hand. Six of those fingers were two feet long and could do serious damage, simply because they were strong and could reach some areas where the other fingers could not.

The teeth on another one were big and looked like rails from a fence. They were sharp at the bottom like someone sawed them into a deadly point. They smelled of puke. Carlie threw up at the smell alone. Their ears were long but did not flop because something occupied them. It looked like thousands of bugs crawling around. The closer one of the bugs got, Carlie could see that they were unlike anything she had ever seen before. They were a dark silver with bubbly eyes and razor-sharp antennas.

They could strike anything if in position. Every few seconds, the things would slap at their ears saying something in a tongue that was unfamiliar to Carlie. The bugs would behave for just a minute or so because they could not wait to get to her. Bisalten would let them know when.

The eyes on Bisalten were hard to look at. It looked like only a face. Its eyes were burnt on the inside. Smoke was coming from them. It blinked almost continuously. Some of the nose, if that was a nose, twitched constantly because something was pouring from it. It looked like mucous, but it was lava like. Carlie was frightened because she could not wake up from this nightmare. Bisalten tried to block her from an entrance that was just big enough for her to get through.

In a distance, she heard little babies coming. They were cooing. Some were angrily crying. They were coming straight for Bisalten and his assistants. There were hundreds of newborns and a few just born babies who were less than an hour old. There were stillbirth babies, aborted babies, and babies that died at the hands of adults.

Why would babies be coming for these things? Carlie did not know that these babies were exclusively for her. For some reason, she felt a sense of relief. She was smiling. Whatever wanted her spirit broken was no longer able to contain her.

Bisalten and his crew were afraid of the babies, rightfully so. They were Heaven sent. Bisalten knew they were on a mission from God and nobody and nothing could stop, touch, scare, or force them away. If they disobeyed just once, they would be removed from the real boss's army. If the babies showed up and told them to leave, they had no choice.

One of the lead babies, who could not have been more than six months old, screamed, "Be gone, Bisalten! You CANNOT have her. LEAVE NOW!"
The three of them disappeared. Where to? Carlie had no idea.

She did not know if she was unconscious or dead. Out of nowhere, a little baby said, "Don't worry, Carlie.

Nothing will bother you anymore. We are escorting you now."

Escorting me where? How and why would babies be escorting me?

She was traveling and could not wake up. Is this a dream? Her eyes were closed but she was awake. She did everything she could to open them but could not. To her surprise, there was a sound in her ears that suggested she was traveling extremely fast, almost unhuman like. The ringing was soft but clear. There was a slight breeze blowing, neither hot, warm, cold, nor cool. The smell was now amazing. She wasn't sure if it was a combination of vanilla and some exotic flower or if it was a mix of a designer perfume so soft and elegant you could only get a whiff of it. Whatever it was, it was delightful!

What did that mean? Was she coming up on a field or something? She noticed that every few seconds or so a bright light would switch on and then off. It was never a dark ride, but a dream that seemed real.

Whitlow

Whitlow was clueless as to just how sick his wife, Centrice, was. All he knew was that he loved her with all his heart. He was determined to love her back to her normal life.

Centrice was diagnosed with stage four cancer just three months before when she was admitted to the hospital while in an unconscious state. It was shocking to her family and friends because she had never been sick a day in her life. Her smile was contagious and her love for humanity was amazing.

While Whitlow sat there and observed his wife's labored breathing, he thought of the day he met her 33 years before.

She was sitting in Central Park in New York City, smiling while reading a book. To this day, he doesn't know where he got the nerve to start a conversation, but he did.

"Is the book that good?" he asked. When she looked up at him, all he saw were the biggest, prettiest brown eyes in the world. Her eyelashes were so long most people thought they were fake. Her skin was so smooth it reminded him of milk. Her hair was parted in the middle. The wind blew through it like a whisper.

He liked her eyes. They were big but almost squinted. Her lips were small, even with the soft red lipstick.

Although her face was round, her hairline was thick and beautiful. It gave her face a more oval shape.

Her teeth made her smile light up a room.

The green jacket she was wearing was boxed at the shoulders and curved at the waist. And those legs! They just sat there, long and smooth.

She was a real beauty.

The excitement in her smile let him know the book must have been good.

She smiled. "Yep. It is good. I'm just finishing up. If you'd like, you can read it. But, quite honestly, I try to discourage people from sharing books because I think it is an injustice to the author. I always suggest that people get their own copy. How about that? I offered the book to you and in the same breath suggested you go out and buy your own copy. I should be ashamed!" They both laughed out loud.

He automatically liked the sound of her voice. It was soft and gentle, and if you looked away while she was talking you could almost feel the smile in it.

"What's the name of the book? I'll get a copy and read it and then maybe you and I can discuss whether I think it is a good book or not!" He laughed again.

"It is entitled, *Almost There, Almost: The Many Faces of Sylvia Traymore Morrison*. I couldn't put it down actually, which is one of the reasons why I just finished reading it. I started on it yesterday."

Whitlow knew then that he was going to not only purchase the book, but that he needed to get her contact information so he could share with her what he thought of the book and take her out.

"Is it okay if we exchange numbers? I'm going to get the book and get back with you so that we can talk about it."

"Sure! I would be happy to hear your thoughts." They exchanged numbers and promised they'd talk soon.

Centrice's eyes followed him as he walked off. Not only was he tall and handsome, he had a rugged, movie star swag about himself. He walked with confidence and the coat he was wearing looked as though it had his name on it. It fit him well.

She remembered the slight dark mustache he had because it fell in line with his smooth lips. She was embarrassed at herself for constantly looking at his teeth, which almost seemed perfect. His light brown skin was so smooth it looked like coffee with cream. She was sure there was a tad bit of sugar in the coffee. She laughed at herself.

What impressed her most was his voice. She already knew she would go out with him.

The Final Leg

The speed of Carlie's trip slowed down just enough for her to be comfortable. Out of nowhere colors began to appear. The first color of orange was vivid, bright, almost blinding and so beautiful it took her breath away. This orange was the most beautiful she had ever seen or not seen. It was a deep glowing that almost sparkled. It could have been a golden orange color, but then again it could have been a red orange.

It was smooth, and moved around in space like a wind but dazzled the mind. You would have thought it was the sun, close, right there for you to reach out and touch. But wasn't the sun supposed to be yellow? The sun had never been that bright of an orange. It almost hypnotized her. It felt like something warm and friendly was dripping into her veins, so she relaxed and let it do its job. The orange color moved into a yellow setting.

The yellow was so spectacular it looked full of round beads and candy, like jewelry. She had never seen a yellow this rich. She felt like closing and opening her eyes. But wait! She could not open her eyes at all.

Some of the yellow beads started separating themselves from the actual color. There were hundreds of big, pretty, yellow beads. At first, they were tiny. Then, the hundreds turned into thousands and then millions.

The beads looked as if they were chasing behind something more exciting than themselves. They casually started mixing with the blues!

There was a multitude of blues that were so deep she wanted to touch them, but realized her eyes were still closed. How on earth was she seeing these beautiful colors with closed eyes?

The blues turned into all kinds of shapes—boxes, squares, rectangles, and triangles. Each shape produced its own blue. The navy blues had what appeared to be noses and mouths, as if they could talk, but they flew by so fast you almost missed them. The other blues changed up with almost every move. The soft blues were almost white with a hint of the same blue in the sky. There were turquoise blues appearing to be water blue blending with clear water. One of the blues wrapped itself around all the blues and then spit them out in a cloud so big and beautiful that it was almost impossible to see the hundreds of different blues. It was amazing.

She had never seen anything like them. But wait. Maybe she wasn't on Earth. Never had she seen colors so magnificent.

After experiencing the reds and greens, and almost being overwhelmed by what they did to her heart and mind, she started wondering where everybody was. Why are there no people on this trip with her?

She heard different sounds from what could easily be little babies again. She thought maybe Bisalten and his crew was returning. She started sweating.

"Carlie, don't be afraid. Trust me. No one will bother you from here on out. We told you that and we meant it."

The babies were cooing and laughing at the same time. Whatever was going on, they loved every single moment. You could hear one baby's coo followed by the most tickled laugh anyone could imagine.

Why were babies in her dream? Who is taking care of the babies? She tried to scream, "SOMEBODY GET THE BABIES!"

She was under the impression that she was the only adult around and couldn't attend to them. Somebody had to help them!

She heard another baby say, in the most adorable and clear baby voice, "We are okay, Carlie! We're having fun and can't wait to meet you!"

How could a young baby who coos talk? She wanted to see them badly, but her eyes were still shut tight. Why couldn't she open her eyes?

She was not in a car, on a train, or on an airplane, so where was she going? The only thing she remembered before this ride was going to sleep while thinking of her totally devastated family. In that moment, the mental pain and grief she experienced before going to sleep subsided.

The ride started to slow down. Her heart started pounding. She did not know where she was nor why. She couldn't reach for anything because she did not know if she had hands or not.

She wondered if she would finally get to find out what all those colors were and why so many babies were cooing and laughing around her. She could not wait to see the babies. Were they really babies?

In Carlie's confusion, she thought maybe she was still asleep, but she could now see. Her eyes opened! She could hear. She could even feel.

It took just a few moments for the ride to come to a halt. She heard one of the babies say, "We're almost there. Almost! All babies get ready. Make sure you all stay together. I'm excited for you!"

All babies get ready? Get ready for what? Everything stopped. Babies were flying past her, laughing and cooing, having the time of their lives. There were hundreds of them. Some were in the group that got rid of Bisalten and his crew. Several of them waved and told Carlie they would see her later.

Those babies can fly and talk? I must still be dreaming. She sat up.

There was a sign in front of her that read, "New Souls – Wait Here for Your Mentor." She was really confused. Was she a new soul? There were people everywhere.

To her surprise, her mother and father were standing in front of the sign smiling with tears in their eyes. A couple of the babies stopped to see them and let them know Carlie had a good ride. They told them about how Bisalten tried to get to Carlie.

Her parents gave her a moment to collect her thoughts. Her mother could not wait to grab and hug her. She was crying with delight.

In Carlie's confusion, she was in tears at seeing her parents, but they were dead.

"Mom, Dad? What's going on? Where am I? How did you get here?"

Her mother was so overjoyed she could not talk. Her father had to say everything.

"We got here the same way you did! Welcome to Heaven, Honey!"

How Could
This Happen?

The sun was quiet. Cars that usually were a part of loud traffic noise were not blowing their horns or moving at jet speed.

The whole world was shocked and mourning as one of the greatest singers of all time was being laid to rest.

Carlie Stetson was being laid to rest too. What was so devastating about this funeral was that Carlie lost her mother and father earlier that year in one of the most horrific car accidents ever. Two months prior to that, she lost Quan, her little 13-year-old brother who was accidently shot in a drive-by. The shooting was listed as mistaken identity. With all the gun violence taking place, it was unfortunate that the gunmen did not identify the correct victim before releasing their deadly bullets.

This series of deaths had Carlie in a state of depression. Losing her little brother was bad enough, but for her parents to die that same year was unbearable.

Many people believe that Carlie died of a broken heart, but medically she simply died in her sleep of natural causes. She was only 27 years old.

Carlie's oldest sister, Shonda, was left to take care of her younger brother, William, who was known throughout the neighborhood as Watty. There was also her little sister, Janiece, who was only 11 years old.

When Carlie died, Shonda was not only devastated but had no idea how she would bury her sister.

Shonda was a short, young woman. She worked out three times a week and anyone who saw her knew that right away. She was muscular yet gorgeous. She wore her hair cropped close to her head. She dyed her hair a light brown, almost blonde, which matched her light brown eyes. Shonda's eyes could melt you. They were so alive and warm you could not help but stare at them.

When Quan died, her parents had no insurance for him, so they took out a second mortgage on their house. The money she received from her parents' life insurance was just enough for Shonda to bury them.

Shonda did not want to ask family and friends for help to bury Carlie simply because they had all been right there helping in whatever way they could throughout the prior three deaths. Everything was just too much. She was drained financially, mentally, and emotionally.

That night, as exhaustion covered her entire body, she prayed.

"Dear Lord,

I come before you with a broken heart. I can hardly breathe. I know that you are doing your work and I know that you won't put any more on me than I can bear. Lord, I am so broken right now. You already know that I must bury Carlie, and I can't even think about anything through all this grief.

I'm going to ask you right now, in the name of Jesus, to help me. Lord, not only do I need a financial blessing, but I need understanding, guidance, and relief from what I am going through. I need to have some of this grief lifted so that I can at least smile for my little sister and brother. I need to know that we will be alright. I'm asking you to bless them right now because I don't know what else to do. I don't know what they are thinking, and I don't know what they are really feeling. If their grief is anything like mine, I am desperately asking you to help them too.

Lord, please. God, please. PLEASE help me so that I can give my sister a decent burial. I'm going to thank you right now in the name of Jesus. God, I need help and I need it bad. This grief is overwhelming and if you don't help me I don't know who will. Thank you, Lord. Amen."

Shonda broke down and cried while still on her knees. She could barely get up to get in the bed. Her tears were streaming, and her throat was thick from grief. It felt like a piece of an apple or something was stuck in her throat. Her eyes felt heavy and half closed. Her nose was running, and her chest hurt. "Nobody can live like this, can they?" she thought to herself. All kinds of thoughts ran through her head. She finally remembered that she prayed. There was basically nothing she could do now.

Finally able to lift herself to the bed, Shonda went to sleep, swollen eyes and all.

When Shonda awoke the following morning, she could hardly see from the swelling of her eyes. She sat up on the side of the bed and took a deep breath. The tears started streaming. She was listening to a voice in her head saying, "You cannot make it through this horror. Both your mother and father died. You lost a brother AND now a sister. Shucks, you know if you want, you can die too and be done with this grief. You won't have to live with this awfulness any longer."

Another voice quickly interrupted, "That's foolishness. What will your younger sister and brother do? If you die, you may as well know that they will die too. Who will take care of them? You must live and be brave for them. After all, you are all they have, and no one will take care of them like you. Stay in prayer, Shonda. Many people are praying for you."

She shook her head no, responding to the thought of suicide. It almost sounded good.

She stood up, headed to the bathroom, and could not believe what she saw in the mirror. She looked like an old woman who had not had any sleep for days. She turned the cold water on and splashed her face several times until it felt like life was re-entering her body.

Spencer

What Spencer did not know was that his wife was preparing to leave. Marlow did not expect to give birth to twins two years ago, and no way was she going to ruin the rest of her life watching after two babies and the two that were already there. She never wanted children in the first place. She always wondered to herself how on Earth she ended up with a man who lost his first wife and had children that came with him. What in the world was on her mind?

Marlow fell for Spencer shortly after she met him. They were both in the bank when she tumbled into him after stubbing her toe.

He turned around and oh goodness! His eyes met hers and he smiled. She apologized and smiled. He smiled back. She saw his perfect teeth and gentle smile and wondered if he was married. His hair was combed with a part and cut to perfection.

She was happy that he was drop dead gorgeous. She was also thrilled that she knew she looked like someone in high fashion.

Spencer was around 6'1" tall and built like he worked out all the time. The suit he was wearing helped too. It was a navy blue Giorgio Armani soft model windowpane suit. It fit him like a glove. She couldn't help but stare at his shoes. They were shiny and smooth. She saw him smiling at her smiling at him.

Marlow was a redhead. Her hair was long and bouncy. She had a mole on the left side of her face that she thought was Marilyn Monroe like. She often saw people from her peripheral vision turn around and watch her. She was wearing a Vera Wang imitation dress that fit her like she was a princess. Her legs were long, and her shoes complimented the red and orange dress perfectly.

Marlow had a voice that matched her attractiveness. Her laugh was unmatched and made others laugh too.

Spencer told her that he would have to charge her for bumping into him; therefore, she would have to go out with him. Marlow did not even hesitate. She gave him her number and they were inseparable from that point on.

They both talked about their past and what the future held for them. She learned about Sasha, Spencer's first wife, and her demise. She felt bad for Spencer, but she was falling in love with him and he was falling in love with her. They got married after a short romance. Marlow accepted that he had sons and prayed that she could one day love them too, but she was just not cut out for that type of life.

Spencer's two boys were a handful. Chester, a bright, sharp 17-year-old played drums in a band and was always beating on the drums in the house. His playing instantly gave her a headache.

Monroe, the 14-year-old, constantly pressed her about going to the library, or any bookstore, because he loved to read more than anything. His library was huge. He was always excited about discussing his latest find. He told her how he traveled the world through books and that most of his friends did not want to hear any of what he was talking about. Marlow always listened, and he adored her for that. She would often pretend that she was listening while saying to herself, "Shut up, for God's sake. Lord have mercy, why won't he go away!"

After living this lifestyle for a while, Marlow knew she had to get out of the marriage one way or another. She loved Spencer, but this was too much. She could feel the boys' grief about their mother. They were never disrespectful to her, but their grief weighed on her emotions.

Their mother, Sasha, must have been a tolerant woman with lots of patience. Marlow saw pictures of her many times and had to admit that not only was she beautiful, but she could sense an air of kindness in the woman's face. Her hair was long and black and curled at the ends. Her smile was subtle and lit up the room. Her eyes were big, dark and baby-doll like. Her lashes were long and curled upward. She was 5'6" tall, thin, and loved to wear soft colors. The more Marlow looked at the picture, the more she thought of Monroe. He was her spitting image.

What Marlow knew of Sasha was that she was a former school teacher and loved children. Year after year, Sasha received several pictures and cards from her students suggesting she was one of the best and most loved teachers around. Nothing pleased Sasha more than going over her students' homework at night and making notes of how she could help them with the problems the next day.

As Sasha worked, she could hear Chester playing his drums. "He's so good on them," she thought. She encouraged him daily to practice and keep up his grades. She could not have been prouder.

Monroe, on the other hand, was her secret weapon. Sasha believed that one day he would be a senator or someone in a powerful position to help people. He was such a good guy. She loved both her boys with all her heart.

Marlow would often hear the boys discussing their mother and a tinge of jealousy would surface, but she would wash away those thoughts by trying to figure out what she was going to do about her situation.

The Jellybeans

Carlie's mom was assigned to show Carlie as much of Heaven as she could, sort of like her Heaven mentor. The first stop was showing the Heavenly mansions of which there were many in their Father's house. Each house could be as big or as small as one wanted. It was just a matter of imagining what she wanted her house to look like.

Once Carlie was done with her selection, she remembered that she always wanted a baby grand piano considering while on Earth she wanted to be a singer. The piano appeared before she could bat an eye. She looked at her house before leaving, realizing she really did not want to leave its beauty. She closed her door and followed her mother.

Carlie and her mom proceeded through the streets of Heaven. It was nothing like Earth at all. The section they were cruising through on foot housed many friends and relatives, some of whom Carlie did not know. "Your Uncle Theo lives right there. He loves his home so much he rarely comes out."

They passed by sections of people who were chatting about their experience getting to Heaven and how they would have never been able to imagine what it was like.

They both stopped as they passed a couple of guys who were singing on the corner. The sound was amazing. The guys tipped their hats and continued singing songs from several countries in different languages.

There were people standing around talking about sections of Heaven they had visited and where they wanted to go next. A couple of ladies talked about jellybeans. "Whatever that meant," Carlie thought.

They walked until they arrived in an area that Carlie's mom could not wait to show her.

And there they were. In their glory. Gorgeous. Breathtaking. Incredible and marvelous. Nothing could compare to their splendor, beauty, and magnificence. Nothing.

There were trillions and trillions of different colors and endless mountains of amazement.

The jellybeans.

They were sitting there, in all their splendor, with thousands of Heaven's occupants looking at them. Some people were weeping, some were staring at them, and some were so in awe they just sat on the ground admiring how powerful just the sight of them was.

The colors of the jellybeans were beyond stunning. Carlie thought the colors were beautiful on her trip to Heaven, but those colors were mildly beautiful compared to what she was seeing in the jellybeans.

She blinked a few times because this had to be a mistake. Are those really jellybeans? You could see them for miles and miles, and then even further out.

As most people who had been in Heaven for a while knew, these jellybeans were one of God's greatest gifts to mankind.

Carlie looked at them wondering to herself if you could eat them. She was too embarrassed to ask right then and there but would ask her mother later in a private conversation.

As she stared at them, Carlie thought of the trees on Earth. She remembered taking a trip with her parents when she was just a little girl and the trees just kept passing. Endless trees. Tree after tree after tree, and that was just in a small area of North Carolina in the United States. The trees were never-ending.

The jellybeans, on the other hand, had their own majesty. To see them was a blessing.

She wondered if the people that were there wanted to get a special inspiration or something? Did they come here to meditate? Why? What do the jellybeans do? She wanted to know why so many people were just standing there observing.

Her mother saw the amazement in her eyes and smiled softly. She gave Carlie a few more minutes to take it all in.

"You have the exact same expression I had when I first saw them. There are so many that only the Heavenly eye can see. The Earthly eye would fight the thought of abundance like that. Their minds would not be able to absorb what is here. It is the same with understanding God's majesty, of which this is a part. When I found out what these jellybeans stood for, I couldn't move for maybe 10 minutes. The meanings behind them are breathtaking. That's why there are so many people here."

"What do they mean, Mom? Why so many jellybeans? Oh, Momma, whatever they represent, it's got to be..."

"Carlie, when your father and I first saw them, he had to comfort me because I could not believe what I was seeing. They are so beautiful, as you can see, I almost passed out.

I want you to look at just a small portion of them before I tell you why they are here.

Do you remember on Earth hearing many people say they knew their loved one was looking down and protecting them?

Remember when I used to say your grandfather was looking over us? Well, he really was. We just did not know the magnitude of what we were saying."

Carlie listened intently.

"Are you ready to know why they are here? I ask because you don't just talk about the jellybeans without preparing a person."

Carlie shook her head with eyes so wide she could hardly hold back her excitement.

"Each one of these jellybeans, every single one that you see and the ones you can't see, represents a prayer request from someone on Earth. People all over the world pray for their loved ones, people in need of help, friends, family, associates, pastors, neighbors, children, hospital employees, people in the hospital, hospice patients, injured people; prayers for peace, love, finances, depression, cancer, disease, animals. Oh, I could go on. There are some people that get prayers sent from all over the world every day.

Look at the jellybeans, Carlie. The blinking ones are from people we know. See the lady right there? The jellybean that's blinking for her is her blessing to bestow.

See the green jellybean blinking? Go get that one."

Carlie got the blinking green jellybean and handed it to her mother.

The green jellybeans represent a prayer request for a financial blessing. The pink ones represent cancer. The purple ones are for lupus. The white ones represent heart disease while the blue ones are for prostate cancer in men. The yellow jellybeans are for depression, and the orange ones can be for ear, eye, and throat issues. The black ones are for specialties and can range in medical problems from issues with knees to feet or hands, diabetes, high blood pressure—you name it. We just have to announce what it is so that the jellybean can do its job.

You also have multicolor jellybeans available when people have more than one problem they are dealing with that may not necessarily be medical.

Let me tell you about the red jellybeans. Have you noticed there are no red jellybeans here? That's because only God Himself can drop a red one. Have you ever seen a horrible accident where a car is crunched to the point where you know whoever was in that car didn't make it? When someone gets out without a scratch, you know it was divinely ordered. That's because God dropped the red one, and He's the only one who can offer that type of miracle.

"Come here, let me show you something."

Carlie and her mother walked to an edge to look at Earth, and they saw Shonda crying.

"Shonda is concerned that she cannot give you a proper burial.

This will be the first jellybean blessing you will bestow on your sister. I want you to watch her reaction once the jellybean reaches her. She prayed for a blessing last night and her prayer will get answered momentarily. It will help her feel so much better!"

Carlie smiled as she held the green jellybean over the area where Shonda was standing and dropped it. It was at that moment that Shonda went to check the mail. The blessing was about to expose itself. They watched Shonda's every move from the time she opened the envelope to the time the expression of disbelief and tears formed.

Carlie and her mom hugged each other while watching Shonda say, "It's a miracle! OMG! It is a miracle!"

"Mommy! She's elated! Look how happy Shonda is. That makes me so joyful. That green jellybean we dropped on her answered her prayer! I think I'm really going to like the jellybeans and the whole idea of being in Heaven! How amazing is this!"

What Do I Do Now?

Shonda was getting no sleep. Her exhaustion was showing in her face. She went to the mailbox to check the mail, which was full of envelopes that contained bills.

She giggled a little when she saw the cell phone bill. It was a shame that phone companies were robbing people with their charges. She looked at all the extra fees that came with having cell phones on the family plan.

Shonda went through several pieces of mail, most of which were advertisements. There was one envelope that made her put all the rest of the mail down. It was a notice from her parents' insurance company.

She carefully opened the envelope because she was not going to be able to handle a note that said they paid her too much money and needed to be reimbursed. Or maybe it was a bill accidentally sent for the quarterly payments her parents made to the company. It couldn't be. The envelope was addressed to her.

She opened it and there were several attachments. A smaller piece of paper fell out of the papers in her hand and onto the floor.

She reached down and picked it up. It was a check, made out to her in the amount of $56,400. "What? OMG! What is this?" Probably some advertisement suggesting that she was approved for a car loan. She was inclined to throw it in the trash, but something made her read on. She almost screamed. She put her hand over her mouth and continued reading with incredible speed.

"The attached will close out the remainder of the insurance payment from the rider in the original policy. As you know, the policy states that if both parents die together a separate check will be issued to you as the beneficiary. Please note that the $57,000 that is being distributed is minus the $600 fees associated with closing this policy.

Should you have any questions, please call us at..."

Shonda stood there in shock. "Oh my God! Oh my God! Oh Lord!" She broke down and cried. Her prayers had been answered. Her financial worries were presently over. She could now bury her sister with respect.

She sat on the couch and cried thankful tears of joy and sadness combined.

Her mother and Carlie were watching the whole scenario.

Prayer

Whitlow decided to go home after having spent the last two nights with Centrice. He couldn't find the strength to leave her with all the heavy heaving and coughing she was experiencing. In just one week she lost eight pounds. She could not eat by herself and therefore was being fed intravenously.

After the nurse convinced him that it was okay to go home, get a shower, and maybe return later, he decided to leave. It would not be good if he ended up sick from worry and emotional strain. The nurse assured him that Centrice would be looked after.

On his way out, he stopped and kissed his wife on her forehead and couldn't help but stare at the shell of a body she had been reduced to. Her hair was gone, her lips were dry, her arms were pure skin, and her face was sunken.

He thought to himself, he would pray for his wife. He had never been a praying man but what harm could it do? After all, at this point, that was the only hope he had. He made a mental note that when the day was over, and he was ready for bed, he would speak with the higher power that everyone was convinced could help him and his lovely Centrice. He could not understand how people could believe in a power they could not see.

All his thoughts in the past were that those people were silly. Praying to a man they had never seen and becoming emotional just because what they prayed for coincidentally came to pass? Yeah, okay. But what else could he do? "Centrice is dying. I will lose the love of my life if I don't do everything possible. If it means praying, even though I don't know that much about praying, I must go for it," he thought.

70,000 Sections

Carlie sat down and looked at her mother. She remembered how much she missed her after she died. That was all she could think of. It was hard for her to sleep at night and her thoughts were of nothing else. The grief was unbearable. Not to mention sometimes when she thought she was grieving for her mother, she was also grieving her father.

In Heaven, that grief was gone. She looked around Heaven and admired its splendor. There is something unusual and magnificent about being here. She could not explain it, but she felt it befitting of what it must be like to be a queen.

She was in awe of Heaven. There was so much of it. When her mother explained that there were over 70,000 sections and each one was enormous, it was hard for her new Heavenly mind to consume.

The next area she visited was amazingly shocking. These people lived on Earth 2,000 plus years ago, and were from the eras many know as A.C.—After Christ and B.C.—Before Christ. It was an open, clearly defined area. There were no modern houses like the people of the current century. No cars or planes or modern technology. It was simple everyday living with nothing extra.

Carlie learned that this portion of Heaven was designed by God for people who wanted to stay in their century parameters. They did not want to move up to current times. However, if they ever wanted to venture into any of the other worlds of Heaven, it was wide open to them.

Carlie was mesmerized at the history associated with this area. Right away, she recognized Julius Caesar who was sitting and talking with several men of historic backgrounds. Spartacus, Richard I of England (Lionheart) who was King of England from July 1189 until his death, and An-Nasir Salah ad-Din Yusuf ibn Ayyub (also known as Saladin) the first sultan of Egypt and Syria and the founder of the Ayyubid Dynasty were laughing and paying close attention to Shinmen Takezo Miyamoto Bennosuke (who some called by his Buddhist name, Niten Doraku, also known as Miyamoto Musashi) because he was a celebrated swordsman while on Earth.

Hannibal Barca and Sun Tzu were playing chess while Leonidis I and Alexandra the Great were looking over what appeared to be a map.

Carlie knew this information and who everyone was because she loved History when she was in school and was fascinated by some of what she learned during her studies. There were obviously people who were well-known in that area of Heaven, including George Washington, the first President of the United States.

None of these historic greats wanted to be a part of the new Heaven of the current era. They were satisfied knowing that if they ever wanted to venture out, it was easy for them to do so. They were enjoying eternity in the timeframe during which they lived on Earth.

The same was the case with Leonardo da Vinci, one of the greatest artists ever. His painting of the Mona Lisa is, to this day, being protected with top shelf security. When it travels to other museums you would think a dignitary was coming.

Carlie saw him looking down on Earth. He was an Italian, she remembered reading, and loved his black cap. His beard was a light brown mixed with blonde. He must have grown the beard for a while because it was long and almost to the middle of his chest. His eyes were wide, but they seemed to squint. His look was piercing but friendly. There was no appearance of a smile and he was rubbing his beard as if he was in deep thought. His clothes were from a different time. Carlie smiled and thought, "This dude is not with the whole tennis shoe movement!" His pants were not hanging down and he wore no jewelry at all. No piercings or tattoos covered him.

His coat was draped around his shoulder like a cape. It was lined with fur around the collar and at the ends of the arms. There were no buttons on the coat but strings that could be tied to keep it closed.

People in Heaven could operate on whatever temperature they chose, and da Vinci liked cold weather. Most people found it amazing that you could adjust your own personal temperature and it would only affect you.

He was standing there looking at a blue jellybean he was holding in between his forefinger and thumb. One of his heirs, generations down, was suffering with prostate cancer. At the time he was on Earth, this disease was unheard of. Carlie walked toward Mr. da Vinci and introduced herself. She told him she knew all about him and was delighted to meet him. Without hesitation, he proceeded to tell her about the blue jellybean.

"My great, great, great—and more greats, which are too many to count, has been praying about his condition so I thought I'd drop a jellybean on him and take away his sorrows, at least until God is ready for him. He has a lot of work to do on Earth and this disease could affect his legacy. You are more than welcome to watch. It is one of the most incredible, fun things to do here in Heaven."

Carlie obliged and watched as the great Leonardo da Vinci dropped the blue jellybean on Earth to land directly on and bless his relative. The doctor walked in almost immediately to speak with da Vinci's relative. Carlie and da Vinci listened, smiling the whole time. They could not wait to see and hear Jimmy's reaction.

"Jimmy, I have some good news for you," the doctor said. "From the looks of things, you are cancer free. I know it's been a long journey and you've been through a lot, but you are clear! I will have the nurse get your release papers."

Jimmy and his family were ecstatic at the news. Tears were everywhere. His children were literally jumping with joy. His wife was crying, and Jimmy was hugging any and everybody. They all stopped to say a prayer and thanked God for the blessing.

Per da Vinci, what he was most delighted with in Heaven were the jellybeans. At any given moment, once the jellybeans were open to Heaven's occupants, they would often go to their offspring, several hundred years down the line, and drop a miracle. Most of the recipients did not know who their ancestors were, but generally screamed with joy when a miracle came through as was the case with Jimmy.

There was nothing, and da Vinci meant nothing, that could compare to dropping a jellybean for not only a loved one but a random person who needed a blessing. When asked if he would like to be returned to Earth to live he said, "No, thank you. If people knew the joy of being in Heaven, they would never, ever want to go back to Earth, even though they miss their loved ones.

Just wait until you see some of what's here. Be thankful that God grew your mind in preparation to exist in Heaven because your Earthly mind would not be able to remotely imagine the majesty of what you are about to experience. Welcome to Heaven, Carlie. You are truly blessed to be here."

Carlie walked away filled with emotion and could not wait until she could drop her first jellybean.

Her mother was waiting and asked her what she thought. She first had to get over the fact that she just met Leonardo da Vinci and watched him drop a jellybean from Heaven to a family member who was several hundred years younger than him. That was amazing. Simply amazing.

Visitors from Heaven

Watty sat up on the side of his bed, sleepy eyed and confused because he just woke up after finishing a conversation with his father. It had to be a dream because his father was dead. It was a blurry encounter and one he vaguely remembered.

His father told him that he and his mom were fine and enjoying Heaven. He told Watty that they were watching over him and although they knew he was sad, not to worry. He should be happy for them.

Watty remembered his father saying something like, "Love on Shonda. She is hurting bad right now. But, given time, she will come around. For now, you are the new man of the house." His father drank some water and told the cow, "Be a good cow." What in the world was that about?

Watty scratched his head. He realized he badly needed a haircut. No one had done anything with anybody since Carlie's death overrode everything. He needed to tell someone about his dream because although it was strange, it seemed real. He was convinced that his father was there visiting him in his sleep and no one could tell him any different. He just wished he knew what the cow was about.

Ooh Those Babies!

Carlie finally walked into the baby area. The babies were waiting there for their next assignment. They were all talking, laughing, and cooing with each other.

Carlie could not figure out why they were cooing when they could clearly talk. She thought it must have been some sort of secret code.

Some of them looked at her and smiled. Others kept talking about their journey to Earth. Several of the babies were just eyes. "How weird," Carlie thought. Eyes? Only eyes? What did that mean?

She walked over to where the first 20 or 30 babies were and spoke. They all spoke back to her in unison. "Hi, Carlie!" She asked if she could join them because there was something special about these babies, especially the ones that were just eyes.

She told them how she just arrived in Heaven and was learning so much. She saw the mansions, which were amazing. Some were so big they would take up two or three blocks on Earth. She soon learned that the Heavenly eye was a lot different from the Earthly eye.

When she spoke about the jellybeans, all 1,000 plus babies gathered around. They were clearly mesmerized by the jellybeans. The one thing they were all looking forward to was having a relationship with all the colors of the magnificent jellybeans.

Every two or so babies, Carlie saw a pair of eyes. Just eyes? The more she looked at them, the more breathtaking they became. There was almost a military feel to them as the eyes searched their surroundings constantly. One could almost not follow their lead because they were checking every single item in their vicinity, down to a piece of dust. They were clearly no nonsense.

An eye would occasionally look at her, and although they could make no expressions she felt the smile. She smiled back.

She respected them. She knew their role was magnificent and important. She just knew it. She wanted to know why they were there, why they were only eyes, and what exactly did they do?

The eyes were serious and put their job on the front line. Carlie forgot she was sitting in Heaven.

The next several sentences would blow her mind.

"When these babies leave Heaven to be created, they are not fully made like you see them here.

We are escorts to the womb. It is one of the top three jobs assigned in Heaven. God takes the babies very seriously.

Whenever God is ready for a newborn to be born, we are assigned to go straight to the womb to protect the creation.

Our job is to be on the watch for anything spiritually unusual that may try to interfere with the creation. Once in the womb, one of us proceeds to the male who has the matching seed to keep watch of his half. We lead that half to the womb and make sure the creation goes through without interference. When everything is in place, both of us are back together as a pair of eyes.

After they have been in the womb for approximately 40 weeks, one of the most special moments of a parent's life is when their baby is ready to leave the womb. We have seen mothers cry and fathers pass out during delivery. We have been with the babies when they are born at a hospital, in the home, in cars, on buses, trains, airplanes, you name it.

Once the baby is out our job is done. We head to our next assignment, which includes picking up babies who did not make it through the process. That could be due to several reasons beyond our control. If a parent is disobedient and puts the unborn in danger, we can't help the unborn.

We also have the job of guiding the babies who must die on Earth back to Heaven. Parents would be shocked to know how happy the babies are to come back. It is so sad when they leave, but we know what is going to happen once they return.

We have seen mothers cry again. We have seen fathers not talk for a long time. We have seen parents falling to their knees asking why.

What they don't know is that the babies are the only species in the entire universe who get to talk with God the moment they arrive back in Heaven. You see, older people do not get to speak with God right away. Those are moments that no one knows about but us – the babies and the babies' eyes.

Did you know that when babies transition back to Heaven, they are groomed to work on red jellybeans that will be used for miracles by God? Only God can drop a red one. These babies are the most well cared for species in Heaven.

The most popular request the babies ask God is to bless their parents, no matter what the case. We heard one baby thanking God for the opportunity to be right there with him. Not one baby, as far as we know, was sad they had to leave Earth.

Another reason we are the eyes is because we are right there on the spot for babies that were not wanted and whose mothers, for whatever reason, had them removed from their bodies without the assistance of God. Most people categorize these as abortions. To avoid the babies that did not make it to full term being sad, he lets us be eyes to guide their little unborn souls back to Heaven.

These babies feel no pain once on their journey to Heaven. If people only knew the devastation they go through prior to going to Heaven, they would sob. However, once they are on their way, God lets us take good care of them while guiding them back to him.

Some of our sad times are when babies are harmed and taken from Earth by heartless grown people. Some babies are shaken or beaten to death. Oh, we could go on and on. God's gift is that He does not let the babies suffer – at all. Instead, they come up here and help God with the jellybeans.

The beauty of it is, all the eyes are incredibly instrumental in the making of lives on Earth who will eventually return to Heaven. It is so amazing that no one wants to go back to Earth because being a baby in Heaven is beyond anyone's imagination. The work we do as eyes is spectacular. And we all, each set of eyes, love what we do. We are the happiest entities in the entire universe. Thank God for the eyes. He always says, 'The eyes have it!'"

Meeting God

There was a group of new adult arrivals sitting in a circle, casually talking about meeting God since they were now in Heaven. Every single one of them gave their rendition of what they thought it would be like.

One guy, who died peacefully in his sleep, said his trip to Heaven was amazing and the colors gave him the impression that he was about to enter the kingdom, as he did. He thought that God would be sitting somewhere waiting for him, he did not know it was going to be a spiritual act. He automatically assumed that God was a man who looked like him.

Another said he thought the colors on his trip WERE God. He did not know what to expect.

One asked what they were supposed to say upon meeting him. "Do you bow down? Do you just shut up and let him talk? Are you allowed to ask questions, or does he already know what questions you have on your mind?

Who goes first with asking questions? Is it like being in a classroom?"

There was one guy, Barbados, who sat and listened to everyone talking. He may have been the only person who did not have a question to ask about meeting God. He observed and listened carefully to every single item that came up in the conversation.

He was a quiet man. He looked like he could have been from an Arab or Latin American country. His eyes and spirit were kind. He appeared to be no nonsense. Fortunately, not one of the people there passed judgment. Their main concern was what happens when you meet God. While there was little anxiety, most were excited and could not wait for the day when they finally went before Him.

Barbados had already visited the jellybeans. He listened to the babies often too. They always fascinated him. He had been to a few other sections of Heaven, but was intrigued by the waterfalls. The sight of some of them twisted his mind because he was completely unable to figure them out. Their beauty and splendor were something to behold.

He was now positioned on the front line to meet God. He didn't know what to think or what he should do. In just a matter of two Earthly days, he would be in front of the throne. He met many people who met God before. Every single one of them was almost unable to speak about their experience.

Barbados died when he was 42 years old. He was in the hospital waiting for a kidney. It never came. Barbados, a man who was unafraid of dying, was a praying man. He was an activist for his people. He and his wife had five children. His oldest son was the spitting image of him and had a similar personality. He too was quiet and unbothered by death. They both wanted to live good lives that impressed God (according to what they believed), then hope for the best.

They lived in the United States right outside of Chicago, Illinois. They left the city and moved to the suburbs because of the violence and killings. The police stopped Barbados' youngest son almost daily. It was routine. Barbados noticed there were no policemen in Heaven. "I guess they won't need them." he thought. There's no danger here, no violence, and no nonsense. There were no ambulances or fire trucks either. Every single person in Heaven had nothing to be angry about or anything to fight about. There weren't, and would never be, any problems whatsoever in Heaven. That was clear and well understood. All Barbados could think about half the time was, "What is happening to my wife and family?" He remained quiet in those thoughts.

Barbados got sick one day on his job. His side was hurting him badly, but he did not want to leave work because he was the breadwinner in his family. He had no room to take off and go to a doctor during work hours. He would have his wife make an appointment for him on the weekend.

The pain went away during the first week. Barbados thought no more about it. The next episode was not as pleasant. He was in such pain that he had no choice but to leave work and have his condition checked.

He was sent home. It was suggested that he see a specialist as soon as possible.

He asked his wife to make an appointment for him, but whenever she suggested a day it was not a good one. Then, Barbados forgot all about seeing a specialist.

Finally, a couple of weeks later, he passed out at his job due to the pain. He was rushed to the emergency room, but the hospital was unequipped to treat him. He was airlifted to an institution that could possibly help him.

After being examined and having many tests, the doctors asked why he had not come in before now. They told him he was in bad shape and there was little hope for him considering he let his condition go without getting help. Less than four hours later, he went into a coma.

Barbados remembered his trip to Heaven. He was afraid the whole time. He did not know if he was headed to Heaven or hell. But, he knew he was on a ride to his eternal destination because he had never experienced anything as beautiful.

However, he knew that the dark side was tricky. They could place beauty in front of you to make you think you were headed to Heaven, and then spill the dark beans with laughter and horror as you proceeded to hell. At least that's what he had been taught in his lifetime.

When he arrived in Heaven, he took a deep breath. All he could say was, "Thank you, God!" His mentor in Heaven was his father. He was so delighted to see him. He tried to be strong and did not want his father to see him cry, so he did everything he could to hold back the tears.

After being shown around a few parts of Heaven, there was still an itch in the back of his mind about his family, especially when he was introduced to the jelly-beans. He wondered why none of his family in Heaven or his ancestors dropped a jellybean on him while he was sick.

Later that day, he received a message that he was a part of the group next in line to meet God. That very message let him know that while there were many jelly-beans on the jellybean mountains for him, God wanted him home. There were assignments God wanted Barba-dos to complete. It didn't matter whether his Heavenly family dropped a jellybean or not. These were God's in-structions.

After only a short while in Heaven, Barbados was mesmerized. Nothing could compare with the splendors of Heaven. However, there were times when he missed his family so much that he decided if he ever got a chance to speak with God, he would ask Him if he could go back home. He loved Heaven, but there was an itch in his heart to return to his family. He was one of few who had that desire.

His chance to meet God was coming up, and all he could do was watch and listen to others. He was so ner-vous about the idea of asking God to send him back that he was almost sick. No one he ever spoke with had a desire to go back, but he missed his family some kind of terrible. He would learn his destiny shortly.

His time arrived.

"Barbados Allahanduh, please come forward."

He stood up.

Walked toward the gates.

He was sweating.

Scared.

Nervous.

Crying.

His tears were never ending.

He was about to meet God Almighty.

He closed his eyes.

Bowed his head.

Cried harder.

"Oh my God! Oh my God."

"God, please! Please."

A door opened.

Barbados stood still.

He could not move.

He looked around, still crying like a baby.

He fell to his knees.

He did not know what to do.

He stayed there and cried and cried and cried.

What would he say?

How would he say it?

Should he get up and walk?

Should he crawl in?

Should he beg for mercy?

Should he ask God about going back?

He could not make sense of anything.

A man came to him.

He asked him to stand.

He spoke to Barbados.

Barbados tried to listen, but he cried and cried and cried.

The man said, "Do not be afraid, Son, for God is God.

He is ready to meet you.

Be ready and honorable.

You will be with him in less than two minutes."

Barbados stood.

He felt like he was in a coma.

He tried to reason with himself.

One minute had already gone by.

God's time is perfect he remembered.

I will meet God in one minute.

The man grabbed Barbados by his arm.

He hugged him.

Wished him well.

Barbados stood.

His hands were at his side.

His eyes were swollen.

His left leg was shaking just a bit.

Before he could figure anything else out, he heard the voice.

It was a deep voice.

It was a kind voice.

It was a stern voice.

Barbados did not see anyone.

He thought he was looking for a man.

He wasn't sure.

He looked around but mostly straight ahead.

There was a transparent cloud in front of him.

He started getting nervous again.

It was Him.

God was in his presence!

Barbados dropped to his knees, again.

He put his face in his hands, again.

He faced the floor, again.

He cried uncontrollably.

God said, "I am that I am.

It's okay my son.

Stand up.

We shall talk.

I already know why you're here.

You want to go back to your family.

Tell me why that should be.

I want to hear your words."

There was a knot in Barbados' throat.

He could not talk right away.

He started crying again.

For Heaven's sake, this was GOD!

He tried to talk, but it just wouldn't come out.

He was finally able to utter a few words.

"God, thank you.

Thank you, Lord.

Thank you for allowing me..."

He broke down again.

God asked him again.

"Why do you want to go back?"

Barbados spoke.

This time with assurance.

He would tell God his reason.

"Lord, I love Heaven. I find Heaven to be extraordinary. I am so blessed to be here. What a privilege to come to Heaven and live in Your kingdom. God, I love You. Always have and always will. I'm not sure if it's because I was only 42 when I died or if it's because I was so into my family. I love the wife You gave me. I love the children You gave me. God, I love life on Earth because of them.

My wife is suffering emotionally. I did not know until recently that she is pregnant with another child that You allowed, Lord. I'm so excited about the baby, but sad I won't be there to witness another miracle.

Lord, God, the sad thing is I love it here too; but, I just want to go back and be with my family. I love You, God, and I will love You through eternity. But, I will only be able to love them in one lifetime, which is counted by years. With You, it's forever.

I know I have a lot of gall to ask You this after You blessed me with coming to Heaven. I know that I could have easily been cast into hell. Please know that I love Heaven. I just want to go back, God."

Barbados was done with his plea.
He had spoken his peace.
He held his head down.
He waited for God's answer.
God spoke.

"I knew you would plead hard. You have been a good son. Job well done. You shall return to Earth for an additional 18 years. Your son will be headed to college. When you return to Earth, you will not remember this conversation. You will come out of the coma you've been in for three weeks.

If you return to Heaven in 18 years, there will be no going back. Understand this, Barbados––at this moment, you are guaranteed to live eternity here in heaven. If you go back, you will not have the liberty of returning automatically. That will all depend on what happens in the next 18 earthly years with you.

In all of eternity, there have been few I have let go back simply because once they are here for a while they never wish to return to the same life they had before.

Be on your way my son. I will be watching you. Pray for your loved ones and know that I am pleased."

In that instant, God was gone. Barbados was stunned.

Before he realized what happened, he was back in the hospital waking up from a coma. His wife was crying hysterically. She knew he had been somewhere but had no idea where.

He held his head because God had not fully removed his experience from his mind.

He held his wife's hand and told her, "Sweetheart, I was in Heaven! I really was. I talked to the babies, and there were lots of jellybeans, and God! I talked to God."

His memory failed him. His wife was looking at him and asked, "What are you talking about, Honey?"

He could not answer her. He fell back to sleep, but this sleep was completely different from the coma. The family was ecstatic. Little did Barbados know that God allowed one of his ancestors to drop a jellybean on him. In that instant, God decided He would return Barbados to Earth. It was all masterful.

Barbados had no memory of sitting with the others who were going to meet God. The people knew Barbados had gone in, but they never saw him return.

Before they could finish up, out of nowhere a door opened and hundreds of young and preborn babies dashed out into the area where they were. Some of the babies stopped to speak with the people and shared how happy they were at the chance to be able to meet with God.

The babies were bombarded with questions about themselves instead of what they should be talking to God about.

The first question someone asked was, "How are you able to talk and you aren't even born yet?" Others asked, "Why do some of you fly?" "How can a newborn walk and run?" "This makes no sense at all," was one of the responses.

The babies all cooed and laughed at what they heard. One older baby, who could have been no more than two months old, told the group, "You will soon find out. These are questions people who have not been to Heaven ask because the human mind cannot consume what it doesn't understand or cannot imagine."

One of the babies shouted, "Let's go, Babies! The jellybeans have been released for our use. Let's get some prayers answered."

They bid their farewell and wished all the people who were on their way to see and meet God a super day. They assured each one they would never have another moment like the one they were about to experience. "Meeting God is everything you could and could not imagine. Just you wait and see!"

What About the Animals?

The entire time Carlie was in Heaven, she thought about the animals and wondered where they were. She was always told that animals did not have souls and therefore did not go to Heaven. In those thoughts, she was sad. She remembered their dog, Sammy, a beautiful black and brown Doberman Pinscher. Sammy was a smart dog and although considered dangerous by neighbors, he may have been the kindest and friendliest dog ever. He may not have looked like it, but he was.

Sammy lived to be a ripe 17 years old in dog years and 92 in human years. He died of natural causes in the family room of her house, right next to her dad where Sammy loved to sit and watch television. His favorite program was Scandal. He would often bark the minute he saw the President. Carlie's dad would always laugh and rub his head saying, "It's okay, Fella. It's just television."

Carlie's mom told her that there is a place in Heaven specifically for the animals. It is beautiful and designed so that the animals can enjoy eternity just like humans.

Carlie made sure she crossed the Heavenly rainbow, just like her mother said, and headed to the left side of the bridge where the light was rich. She was supposed to know right away, once she saw the light, that the animals would be there.

Carlie could not wait to get to the animal side of Heaven so that she could look for Sammy. The one thing he always did whenever she came to her parents' house was run around in circles the minute he saw her. You could hear and see the sheer joy of him being in her presence. They practically grew up together and she always felt like Sammy was her little brother.

She remembered the first time she saw Sammy. He was just a baby and the cutest two-month-old dog she had ever seen. The first thing he did was cuddle up to her foot. He did not want to leave. She fell in love instantly.

One of her fondest memories of Sammy was a day she took him out for a walk, keeping him close to her. At that time, he was almost a year old. He was getting big and beautiful not to mention protective.

There was a loose pit bull in the neighborhood and it was coming straight for Carlie and Sammy. Sammy softly growled. It was the first time she heard him in what she felt was protective mode. It must have been dog talk because the pit bull stopped about 10 feet away and Sammy let him have it with his barking. It was loud and demanding as if to say, "Get on about your business!" Sammy walked closer to him, but the bull walked on.

Sammy walked back close to Carlie and was practically leaning on her. She rubbed him on the head and said, "Thank you, Sammy. Good boy!"

Carlie arrived at the front gate of the animal section and low and behold, there was Sammy standing there wagging his tail! He looked young and vibrant as if he just had a fresh bath. He was barking uncontrollably as if to tell her to come with him. He was backing up and spinning around in circles. She burst out crying. "Sammy! OMG! Look at you! I've missed you so much." Sammy was crying and jumping to see her.

Once inside the animal territory, she could not believe her eyes. Thank goodness, they were Heavenly eyes because Earthly eyes would have never been able to see the magnitude of the animals in Heaven.

Centrice

Whitlow was sad these days. His thoughts often surrounded life without Centrice. They were thoughts that took the wind out of him. How would he be able to go on without her?

He was praying often. Usually, he would pray right before he went in with Centrice for her chemo treatment. Centrice would smile and simply say, "Thank you."

She was trying to be strong, but this disease was wearing on her. She knew that if she ever got over this and her cancer went into remission, she would be thankful; however, the anxiety of it returning was simply overwhelming. She already knew if it came back she would not go through this again.

The one thing that got her through was Whitlow. He always took good care of her even when she was in the best of health. She had no children and no siblings. Her parents died years ago. Her other relatives were few and distant.

One evening, a nurse witnessed Whitlow getting a tall glass of ice water for Centrice and setting it on the table next to her bed. That one act that Whitlow did every night always made Centrice feel better.

Centrice often stared at the glass of water when Whitlow sat it down. No matter how tired or weary he was, he always made sure to place the water there. Centrice was waiting for Whitlow. He had not called or come by for a visit.

Tonight, Whitlow did not bring Centrice a glass of water. He died earlier that morning from a massive heart attack.

Hold On, Marlow !

Marlow's patience was running short with Spencer. She was annoyed with Chester and Monroe because those two did whatever the heck they wanted.

The drums were driving her crazy and Chester played constantly. That was basically the only thing he did outside of school and studying. Chester was a good son. He helped around the house too. No one ever had to worry about taking the trash out or cutting the grass. Those were his specialties.

His other specialty was smoking weed. Chester thought no one knew about his little secret, but he was like a zombie when he smoked. Spencer did not know the difference, but Marlow knew. She would often sneak into his stash and roll a few joints herself.

As far as Monroe, she simply disliked him. His reading was short of making her sick. She thought it was a good thing he read, but that's all he did. He was not interested in anything else other than stories.

Marlow decided that there was not enough room in "her" house for all the books Monroe collected, so she decided it was time to clean up and get rid of most of them. Besides, Monroe already read them, and they were just sitting around.

She packed 17 large boxes of books, put them in the family truck, and proceeded to take them to their favorite donation center. She stopped at the corner where there was a four-way stop sign and reached into her purse for her phone. She did not see the truck behind her flying to the intersection where she was stopped.

The truck slammed into the back of her truck pushing it out into the intersection where another car hit the driver's side crushing the entire side where she was sitting. All three drivers were either unconscious or dead. The only person nearby who could call for help happened to be sitting outside on his front porch reading. He not only heard the noise from the slam, but saw the whole incident. Monroe ran into the house for his phone, dialed 911, and rushed to the scene of the accident to see if Marlow was okay. He learned CPR in school and began its administration to her. He wanted her to live and he was going to do everything he knew to help.

He knew she did not care for him much, but this was serious. There was no time for any negative thoughts. Her life was in danger. There was no time for favorites, a like or dislike game. This could be life or death.

What no one knew at the time, including Marlow, was that she was pregnant with another set of twins.

Heavenly Events

There were so many sections in Heaven that a person could get stuck in one section for who knows how many Heavenly years. Considering Earth years were no comparison to Heavenly years, no one paid attention to time.

Occasionally, God would put together an event to welcome people. It is the most amazing networking event you can imagine, almost indescribable.

This event would be for the musicians. Some of the greatest singers in the world who are now in Heaven perform at the concert.

The concerts that God puts on you would never see anywhere in the universe. Those associated with the concerts are historical names, but whether you have heard of them or not, their talents are so ferocious you are thoroughly entertained.

Each concert is different and mesmerizing. Carlie was looking forward to her first concert and thought about some of the people that died before her. She would love to connect with them.

She remembered Rainey, a little girl who lived on her block and died when a car struck her. She went to the book to find out what section of Heaven Rainey was in and low and behold, there she was, right next door! She could not wait to see her.

Carlie also wanted to see her friend Tango, who was killed in a drug raid. Tango was a street guy and was trying to get out of the life he was in. He hated watching his back and trying to keep himself in the clear.

She looked him up and his name was not in the book. She asked around about names that were not in the book and the news was not good.

If you were not listed in the book, you were not in Heaven. What did that mean? Where were they? She made a mental note to ask God about Hell when she met with him.

She thought about other friends and family who died before her and decided after she hooked up with Rainey, she would make a list of all the people she wanted to see. Prior to that, she wanted to find out what happened to Tango. That was weighing heavy on her heart.

Marlow and Her Babies

Hospital personnel were all over Marlow trying to save her and her babies' lives. Code blue was call immediately upon her arrival from the air lift.

Monroe was right there waiting for his father to arrive. He was a minor and personnel could not discuss Marlow's condition with him. What they did tell him was that had he not acted when he did, Marlow would not have made it. Time was of the essence in her case. She would have died from blood loss had she not received attention immediately.

He felt bad for Marlow, and his father was feeling even worse. When he spoke to his dad, he could tell from his voice that he was devastated. He simply could not lose another wife. Spencer started praying immediately. He loved her so much and could not bear the thought of her dying and leaving him.

Spencer ran down the hall toward the ICU where Marlow was being cared for. He asked the nurse if he could see her. She gave him his instructions and tried to prepare him for what he was about to witness. The nurse informed him that they believed both she and the twins would be okay.

Twins? The twins were in the accident too? He was confused because he was told there was no one in the car with Marlow. When the nurse informed him that Marlow was pregnant with twins, Spencer could not move! Pregnant? Twins? What do you mean? We don't know anything about twins.

The nurse sat him down before he went in and let him know that Marlow was only five weeks pregnant. It could very well be that she did not know either. The good thing was, the babies were safe and it looked like Marlow was going to pull through. The nurse said to him, "Somebody upstairs must really like this woman!"

Marianne – Marlow's Mother

Marianne had been watching over Marlow ever since Marlow was 22 years old, the same year Marianne died.

While roaming Heaven, she got word that someone sent a prayer up for her daughter. She headed straight for the jellybeans to see if that prayer released a jellybean for Marlow.

Marianne knew that Marlow was not fond of her adopted kids, yet she could not understand why. She did not raise Marlow to be selfish nor mean, but that's how she was being in this situation.

To Marianne's surprise, the jellybean was there. She also noticed that Sasha was standing right there too. The jellybean was sent by Monroe! It happened to be a tri-colored jellybean because Monroe not only prayed for Marlow, but once he found out about the twins, he prayed for them too. God immediately assessed the prayer and allowed Marianne to deliver the blessing.

Marianne asked Sasha if she would like to be present when she dropped the jellybean on her daughter. With a smile, Sasha bowed her head and motioned as if to say, "Of course." She wanted her Earthly family to be happy, healthy, and relieved that Marlow would be fine.

By the time Spencer got to see his Marlow, Marianne and Sasha were dropping the jellybean on her. Marianne cried when she saw Marlow stirring around. She was going to be fine.

Spencer, on the other hand, broke down in tears seeing Marlow smile. He grabbed her hand and told her not to scare him like that again. He thought he'd lost her, but what a soldier she was. Sasha quickly crossed his mind and he remembered the devastation he experienced when he lost her.

Marlow told Spencer that as she was coming to all she could think of was her mother. It was as if her mother was there with her. She also felt Monroe was there too. She burst out crying. "I've been so nonchalant with Monroe. I hardly ever sit with him while he reads, and he is always so kind to me. Where is he?"

Spencer got up, went to the door, and summoned Monroe to Marlow's room. She surprisingly asked him for a hug. Monroe, confused and shocked, obliged. Marlow had never, ever hugged him or showed any signs of love.

A picture of Sasha's face crossed Marlow's mind as she hugged Monroe. A tear slipped down her face. This was weird.

Marlow thanked Monroe for his part in saving her life. She asked him if he would mind reading to her that evening before she went to sleep. He was ecstatic because he knew just the book he would read to her. It was an autobiography written by a comedienne named Sylvia Traymore Morrison entitled, *Almost There, Almost: The Many Faces of Sylvia Traymore Morrison*. He could not wait!

Spencer asked Marlow did she know that she was carrying twins? She stopped everything, hesitated, and a tiny frown covered her face. She looked around in shock and asked was he serious? She had no idea what he was talking about. "What are you saying?" she asked.

Spencer told Marlow what the nurse told him. He was so happy he was still in tears.

Something changed. The accident. She reflected on her thoughts before it. She wanted to leave home? Was she serious? She could not imagine leaving her family. What was wrong with her for even thinking something so farfetched? Had she really been that selfish? Maybe she was sick and did not know it.

She looked at Spencer and broke down crying.

After what she had been through, she wanted to mend what she had been feeling about her family. She wanted to build a better relationship with Chester and Monroe.

To think that she would now have two sets of twins was incredible. She hugged Spencer with all her might and told him she wished her mother was there to witness it all. However, she knew her mother was watching over her. Little did she know that her words were truth. She kindly whispered, "Thank you" to Heaven and thanked God over and over. It was a good moment.

Marianne and Sasha hugged each other. That jellybean did the trick.

Sasha looked at Monroe and Chester and smiled with pride. They were going to be just fine. Marlow finally came around.

It was time for her to move on and drop a few more jellybeans. She would check back on the boys every day.

Evelyn

Centrice had been through quite a bit in her chemo treatments. She did not know yet that her Whitlow was gone. The doctors did not want to tell her until she was a little stronger. They were shocked when the team went to check on her that morning because she was sitting up.

She told the team that sometime during the night she no longer felt feverish nor was she nauseous like she had been.

She asked if anyone talked to Whitlow because it appeared, from the glass of water not being on her table, that he not only did not come by but there were no phone calls.

The lead physician sat down on the side of her bed and told her what happened. "Your husband died yesterday morning from a massive heart attack. We couldn't tell you because you were almost in an unconscious state and we did not want to send you into any unnecessary shock. I am so sorry for your loss."

Centrice just sat there and stared. She thanked the doctor for letting her know. She wondered if perhaps

Whitlow's energy poured into her body and maybe that's where she was getting this newfound strength.

What she did not know was that Evelyn, a great-great-grandmother of hers on her father's side knew of all the prayer requests Whitlow sent. She was proud of the life Centrice and Whitlow built and was thrilled she would be able to drop a jellybean. It was just a matter of time for Centrice.

Evelyn could not wait for Whitlow to be with her to show him how the jellybeans worked because Centrice needed a blessing right then and there. Evelyn dropped the jellybean on her that night, and it replenished her body with healing.

Centrice did not know exactly what it was that helped her feel better, but she said a quiet prayer and thanked God for the blessing. She was feeling empty and she missed her husband, but she would give him a beautiful going home service.

By the time Centrice got Whitlow buried and all his business taken care of, she went into a state of depression. She wasn't sure what else she was supposed to do while on Earth. She prayed about deliverance and asked for a sign.

Just when she thought she could not live any more, on her way home from one of her doctor's appointments she met a woman who seemed depressed about her cancer. Centrice found herself sharing her story with this woman. She told her how for a while she felt there was nothing else for her to live for considering her husband was gone; however, she knew regaining her health was nothing short of a miracle. It was as if someone dropped a healing agent from Heaven on her behalf.

Centrice saw the woman's eyes light up when she told her that one night she just started feeling better. She spoke of how she was well enough to bury Whitlow.

The story was so inspiring that the woman asked Centrice if she would come to her women's group to speak with them. Centrice obliged and found her new niche. At that engagement, several offers were made for her to speak at the church some of them attended. Each time she spoke, she was invited elsewhere.

Centrice became a life coach and speaker to groups across the country. Her story was told by many and talked about wherever she went.

Every night before she went to bed, she prayed and thanked God for her new life. She missed Whitlow terribly but knew he would be proud of her accomplishments.

She knew that one day she would meet up with Whitlow; but, until then, she smiled at all the help she was giving others.

These nights she would get her own water, take a sip, and get lost in thought. She got tickled at herself one evening because after a sip, she looked around to make sure no one was watching, and slowly lifted her hand as if to wave at Whitlow and let him know she knew he was watching over her. He was. More than anything he wanted her to be happy while he was helping in Heaven.

Carlie's Dad

Carlie felt it was good to sit down with her dad. He was a good listener and always made her dig deeper into her thoughts.

He explained to her how people in Heaven can visit a person's dream when they are asleep. He visited Watty recently. He knew that seeing and speaking with him would lift his spirits.

Watty was not the first person he visited. He and his great-grandfather visited Shonda a couple of weeks before. Shonda never said a word to anyone about her dad's visit because she did not know who the other man was in the dream. She was a little unsure of why her father was visiting, but she was glad to see him.

"I told Shonda that everything was fine and that her mother and I were enjoying the beauty of Heaven. I explained to her that I had not met God yet, but I was on the list to see him. I showed Shonda one of my favorite places in Heaven. I took her on a journey, which was blurry to her, and she could barely remember it. She saw some parts of the jellybean section, but of course thought it was a weird situation, as was the case with her brother and the cow.

My Brother's Keeper

He was running toward her. There was something familiar about him. He looked like her brother, but it could not be. Her brother was only 13 when he died. This guy had to be at least 35 or 36 years old. She saw him, but was it him?

He stopped in front of her.

Looked at her with moist eyes.

Smiled.

Grabbed her.

Gave her a big hug.

Started sobbing.

Said her name over and over.

"Carlie! Carlie! OMG! Carlie!

You are here, Carlie!

I'm so happy to see you.

Mom and Dad are here too."

He let her go and held her by her shoulders. Stared at her and cried.

She was in shock.

How is this older man her brother?

She knew it had something to do with the wonders of Heaven.

How is he now a grown man?

Had to ask.

So handsome.

So manly.

So happy.

So good to see him.

So refreshing.

So intriguing.

So my little brother.

All grown up.

Where did 23 years go?

HE WAS 13 when he died!

Bullets blew his chest open.

You can't even tell!

He's built.

Looks strong.

Heaven is amazing!

OMG!

"Quan, oh my goodness, you look amazing. I'm so happy to see you. Mom said you were here but all over the place. She said you love Heaven and had no desire to be back in an Earthly state!

Okay, okay, wait. How is it that you died when you were 13 years old and you're how old now?"

"I'm 37 Heavenly years old. Mom didn't tell you about that section of Heaven? It is the coolest part of Heaven if you ask me. You can go there and be younger or older. All you have to do is think it and it is on!

I was 52 years old for about three weeks. It was a wow three weeks too. I went through 39 years in three weeks. It was amazing! I'm trying all kinds of ages. I like this 37 number. I'm going to try 82 years old out when I'm done with 37.

So, Carlie, what happened to you? What made you come here? In other words, how did you die?"

"I just died in my sleep. I was so depressed. I could not, or should I say would not, eat and I definitely could not sleep. The thought of you, and Mom, and Dad overwhelmed me daily. I cried most of the time and I struggled with depression. I thought of suicide, but I am not cut out for that. I was too scared. I went to sleep one night and did not wake up in an Earthly state.

It was weird how I got here. I did not know if I was dreaming or in real life during that trip. I saw some ugly beings and then I saw colors. I guess what really impressed me were the babies. They were amazing! How did you get here?"

"I got here like that too. I think everybody travels to Heaven in that same sort of way. I have talked to people who were born in the years before Christ and their experience was almost the same. Did you know you can live in their time era as well? Man, Heaven is too incredible for the Earthly mind to handle. There is so much to do and explore here, it is unbelievable. No matter what your taste, desire, ambition, love, whatever, there are sections that will absolutely blow your mind. You do not have time to dwell on the horrors of what happens in an Earthly life."

"So, Quan, have you met God yet?"

He stopped everything.

That question was electrifying.

Quan broke down in tears.

He was speechless.

God.

My God.

Yes.

He met God.

He stared into space.

Tried to talk.

He could not.

He looked at her.

He looked away.

He cried hard.

He tried to explain the majesty of it.

It took moments before he could respond.

"Carlie, I do not even know what to say. You automatically drop to your knees, not because you are supposed to but because of its intensity. We are talking God here. The Almighty. The Alpha and Omega. The Beginning, The Creator, The... oh, I could go on and on.

Quan stopped.

Hesitated.

Looked at her.

Shed more tears.

Rubbed his nose.

Wiped his eyes.

One hand covered his face.

He cried and smiled at the same time.

He did not say another word for two to three minutes.

"Meeting God is unexplainable. There are no words to tell you because you will have your own experience based on your life on Earth. He already knows everything about you. When I tell you everything, I mean everything.

He asked me about my short 13 years on Earth and if I was sad to be in Heaven considering I was so young when I left. He asked me about the time I tied the rope around the cat's neck. You know, the one that belonged to Mrs. Harris down the street? The cat that I killed? He knew why, but he wanted me to explain to him what prompted me to do that.

I am telling you, I was so nervous because even though our family did not go to church a lot, I thought that whatever I said might make him cast me into Hell. I was so nervous. I broke down and cried right there before him. I was on my knees sobbing.

He told me to stop crying. He wanted an answer from me. I stopped crying and told him why I think I did it. I could not even look at his presence as I talked. By the way, I never saw him in the flesh. It was like a Spirit.

I was so ashamed about killing that cat.

I said, 'Lord, God, I was only 10 years old and acting like a 10-year-old I believe. I thought it would be fun. That's the truth, God. I wanted to see that little cat's reaction. I did not know the magnitude of what I was doing. At that time, I really did not care. I swung that cat around and around until he stopped squirming and howling. I did not understand the true meaning of evil at that time.

I was having fun.' I started crying and kept saying I was sorry. I asked him, 'Please forgive me. Please.'

Do you know what God said to me then?

He said he was happy I was sorry. He said he remembered the night before I died, I thought about that cat. And right before I went to sleep, I said in a whisper that I was sorry for the cat. He was happy that I was remorseful.

He also told me that the guy that shot me was an angry person and that one of our uncles four generations past wanted to drop a jellybean on the guy with the gun so that I would not die due to mistaken identity, but there were no jellybeans for me at that moment. God said he wanted me here, so it happened.

Carlie, the best thing that could have happened to me was coming to Heaven. If people only knew the glory and majesty associated with being here, they would want to come here immediately.

Of course, I was a little sad when I looked down and saw Mom and Dad in a state of depression when I died. Do you remember the day you asked the two of them if they were still grieving for me and Mom said it was not as bad as it was when it first happened? That is because I had the pleasure of dropping a jellybean on them both to remove some of the grief.

It helped them both a lot. Remember, whenever you drop a grief jellybean, it does not remove the grief, but it lifts quite a bit of it so that your loved one can move on. It's just amazing."

Carlie and Quan talked a little more about some of the other sections in Heaven and promised they would see each other as much as they could. Quan said when he went back to being 13, he would be sure to stop and see her.

He left, as she watched him drift into the Heavenly arena of the section she was in. She smiled.

Carlie sat there for a moment.

Decided to revisit the jellybean section.

Nothing like the jellybeans.

They were amazing.

Were the jellybeans open to her?

She wanted to see.

She got up.

She loved the jellybean section.

They were Heaven's greatest gift.

Other than meeting God.

She could not wait for that meeting.

Angels to Earth

On her way to the jellybean section, Carlie saw a large group of people preparing for a trip. Evidently a few thousand people were selected to go back to Earth to speak with people who were 50/50 on the Heaven or Hell side. Their visit could be a determining factor as to those people's fate.

Carlie stopped to chat with a few of the travelers and learned that most of them had no desire to return to Earth; however, when God gives you an assignment, it's a done deal. Besides, they would not be visiting their loved ones, they would visit complete strangers to find out who they really were.

There was an angel by the name of Ausa who seemed nervous. Since her promotion to angel, it would be her first time returning to Earth to confront a living human. She was worried she might give her identity away, which could possibly discredit her from ever having the opportunity to do this assignment again.

Carlie learned that they were both born in the same year.

"I died in a freak accident on a sidewalk. I simply fell and hit my head, and the next thing I knew I was standing there looking at myself laying on the sidewalk. It was weird because I did not feel any pain. I just stood up and there I was still laying on the ground. At first, I thought it was an out-of-body experience.

The next thing I knew, my eyes closed. Just that simple. I was taking a trip somewhere and could not make sense of anything, especially those darling little babies who were cooing and laughing during the trip. I did not know what was going on. One of the babies, who could talk, told me he was my little brother and he would explain it later. I found that strange as well.

When I got to my destination, I saw my grandparents smiling at me. It occurred to me at that moment that I'd died and was in Heaven. Seeing my grandparents again was the best thing to ever happen to me. They raised me from the day I was born because my mother left me with them. It's a long story.

When I was given this assignment, I thought it was kind of cool because I get to see people's real reactions to real situations.

I have five people I'll visit while on Earth. I'm so excited. I will also have an extended conversation with one of them, and the other four I'm not sure. I'm really looking forward to it."

Carlie and Ausa talked about how exciting this was and how this must be one of the coolest assignments in Heaven, other than distributing jellybeans.

Carlie bid Ausa farewell and wished her all the best.

Mother! Oh Mother!

Before Ausa could say or think another word, she found herself on Earth on a busy downtown street in Baltimore, MD. She was holding a sign that read, "Please help me. My children are hungry." Every two or three people dropped change into a bucket next to her foot. She said, "Thank you," and continued to hold the sign.

One woman walked up to her and asked, "Where are your children?" Ausa had no clue, but her finger pointed to two children lined up against the wall who also looked weary and worn. Wait a minute, they were on the trip with her when she first arrived in Heaven! They were two of her escorts! She smiled, and they returned her smile.

"Here, take this and get them something to eat." As she was handing Ausa the money, a man walked by and said in a loud voice, "She's a fraud! I see them out here every day begging for money. She needs to get a job."

Ausa looked at the man who she had never laid eyes on a day in her life. She shook her head as if she could not believe him.

The woman paid him no mind. She started a conversation with Ausa.

"Where are you from?"

"I'm from here."

"My name is Lanette. You kind of remind me of myself. I had two children at one time myself. I was so far gone out here in these streets that I dropped them off at my parents' house and never went back to see them.

I just hope you don't go down the same road I went down. Now that I have myself together and I'm clean, I miss those babies with all my heart.

I just learned the other day that my daughter died on the streets. She fell and hit her head and never recuperated. She and her brother shared the house after my folks died. They raised them both. I'm kind of glad they were not around for my daughter's death. That would have killed the two of them."

Lanette looked far off in deep thought.

"My son is a lawyer. I never got a chance to see either one of my children since the day I left. I want to visit him, but I don't know what he will say or how he will feel."

"I'm sorry for your loss. What were your parents' names?"

Ausa stood still. She was almost shaking at the thought that this could be her mother. OMG!

When Lanette said their names, Ausa had to do everything in her Earthly power to maintain her composure. She was right. It was her mother.

Lanette was pouring out her heart. "I have been out on the streets for a long time. I have also been praying to God every single day to help me get myself together.

When I saw you, I thought of my daughter. You remind me so much of her. Do me a favor. Whenever you can, say a prayer for Lanette. Maybe if God hears one of his less fortunate praying for me too, maybe, just maybe, he might bless me and help me get my life together." She walked off.

Ausa stood there in tears. That was her mother, the woman who birthed her. She was touched by her humbleness. She knew when she got back to Heaven she would ask to check the jellybeans and use one for her. She was not angry at her mother and wanted the best for her. She found it amazing that her mother had no idea she had just finished a conversation with the daughter she missed so much.

She smiled and realized just how good God is. He let her come specifically for this purpose.

The two children sitting up against the wall told Ausa it was time to move on so that they could head back to Heaven. This time she did not need an army of babies. She was already cleared to enter Heaven; however, the two children were there to make sure nothing went wrong on her return.

Ausa was excited to return to Heaven. After all, Heaven is simply awesome. She looked forward to visiting the jellybeans, and quietly thanked God for the jellybeans and the babies.

In the meantime, Thomas, another angel, was on an assignment that involved road rage. His current Heavenly assignment documented people and their habits while driving. That was it.

Before he could get into his car, he heard screaming coming from a car on the road a short distance away. A guy was holding his middle finger up to a person driving a car beside him. Apparently, the other driver was trying to get over to make a right turn, but the angry driver was not about to let him. Why not? Neither of them knew.

Thomas documented the entire scene. He could not understand why such a simple three second act of kindness turned into verbal turmoil on one man's part. How much harm could it have done to let the man over to make the turn? Was the other man aggressive? Was he impolite? Was he disrespectful? What would make someone not want to simply let someone over? He knew right away it was going to be a long day.

He turned around and looked at the two babies sitting in his back seat disguised as his children. He smiled. They smiled back. He loved the baby angels. They were amazing.

All the other angels arrived at their respective assignments accompanied by the babies in some form or fashion. Each one could not wait to get back to Heaven.

Upon Ausa's return to Heaven, she was delighted that the jellybeans were open to be used. She thought about Lanette the entire time and knew that the minute she could she would look for a jellybean prayer from her.

It was never hard to find a special jellybean. All you had to do was search for a person's name and you would be led directly to their prayer request.

She found Lanette's and examined it for a moment. She thought about the little time she spent with her and wished that she could have exposed who she was; but, it was not part of God's plan.

In the meantime, Lanette was sitting on a bench in the local park thinking about the young woman she met earlier. "Wouldn't that be something if that young woman was my daughter? She even looked a little like me," she thought.

She decided to walk back to where the young woman was only to learn that she and her two children, who looked like Lanette too, were gone.

She sat down again and cried. Somehow, she knew that young woman was sent to her. She didn't know how or why, but that was by no means a coincidence.

One day she would find her. In that moment, she felt a change come over her. She wanted to do better. She wanted to change her entire lifestyle. She would do that. She was up and off trying to figure out how she would start her new life.

It was at that moment that Ausa dropped a jellybean on her. Ausa smiled and knew that her mother would be just fine.

Lanette saw her friend Reginald on the way home. He offered her a "good time" with the drugs he was holding. Lanette had no desire for the drugs. In that moment, she knew that something or somebody helped her. She was done with her old lifestyle.

She bid Reginald a good day and smiled at the Heavens. "Thank you, God. I don't know what you did, but thank you."

Conclusion

Most of the characters in this story, through time and experience, could move on and live. It was because of their loved ones who dropped jellybeans and reviewed their prayers that they could flourish the way they did. There are still trillions of jellybeans in Heaven, and there always will be as long as the earth exists!

About the Author

Originally from Washington, D.C., and currently residing in Maryland, Dr. Sylvia Traymore Morrison is the first renowned African American Female Impressionist in the history of this country.

Since impressively hosting *Roast of the Champ* for Muhammad Ali at the legendary Apollo Theater, Sylvia has worked as an associate-writer for *Saturday Night Live*, performed with countless entertainers including Whitney Houston, and released her first book, based on her life, entitled *Almost There, Almost: The Many Faces of Sylvia Traymore Morrison*.

She recently received her first honorary doctorate degree. Sylvia was also honored at the Indie Author Legacy Awards where she received the 2017 Maya Angelou Lifetime Achievement Award.

After 50 years of being in the entertainment business, Sylvia continues to perform and grace stages around the country.

To connect, contact Sylvia at
sylviatraymore@gmail.com

purposely created
PUBLISHING

CREATING DISTINCTIVE BOOKS
WITH INTENTIONAL RESULTS

We're a collaborative group of creative masterminds
with a mission to produce high-quality books to position
you for monumental success in the marketplace.

Our professional team of writers, editors, designers,
and marketing strategists work closely together to ensure
that every detail of your book is a clear representation
of the message in your writing.

Want to know more?
Write to us at info@publishyourgift.com
or call (888) 949-6228

Discover great books, exclusive offers, and more at
www.PublishYourGift.com

Connect with us on social media

@publishyourgift

CPSIA information can be obtained
at www.ICGtesting.com
Printed in the USA
BVHW04s2150050418
512465BV00001B/36/P

9 781947 054820